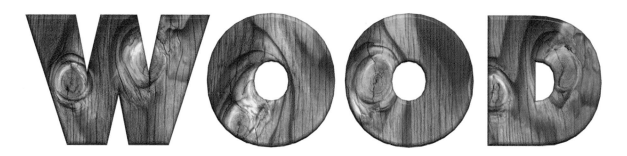

Please visit our web site at: www.garethstevens.com
For a free color catalog describing Gareth Stevens Publishing's
list of high-quality books and multimedia programs,
call 1-800-542-2595 or fax your request to (414) 332-3567.

Library of Congress Cataloging-in-Publication Data

Parker, Steve.
    Wood / by Steve Parker. — North American ed.
        p. cm. — (Science files. Materials)
    Includes bibliographical references and index.
    Summary: Explores the many uses of wood, from paper and cloth to chemicals to works
of art, discussing how wood is processed for these different purposes and how we can help
protect this valuable resource.
    ISBN 0-8368-3087-3 (lib. bdg.)
    1. Wood products—Juvenile literature. 2. Wood—Juvenile literature. [1. Wood
products. 2. Wood.] I. Title.
    TS843.P33   2002
    620.1'2—dc21   2001054227

This North American edition first published in 2002 by
Gareth Stevens Publishing
A World Almanac Education Group Company
330 West Olive Street, Suite 100
Milwaukee, WI 53212 USA

Original edition © 2001 by David West Children's Books. First published in Great Britain
in 2001 by Heinemann Library, Halley Court, Jordan Hill, Oxford OX2 8EJ, a division of Reed
Educational and Professional Publishing Limited. This U.S. edition © 2002 by Gareth Stevens, Inc.
Additional end matter © 2002 by Gareth Stevens, Inc.

David West Editor: James Pickering
David West Designers: Rob Shone, Fiona Thorne, David West
Picture Research: Carrie Haines
Gareth Stevens Editor: Alan Wachtel
Gareth Stevens Designer and Cover Design: Katherine A. Goedheer

Photo Credits:
Abbreviations: (t) top, (m) middle, (b) bottom, (l) left, (r) right

AKG Photo: 14.
Ardea: Jean-Paul Ferrere (8m); Peter Steyn (24–25t).
The Art Archive: British Museum (26t); Eileen Tweedy/British Museum (18bl).
Bridge of Weir Leather Company Ltd., Scotland: 21bl.
Courtalds: 23m.
Mary Evans Picture Library: 22t.
Robert Harding Picture Library: cover [tl], 4tl, 5tr, 6, 6–7, 8bl, 9br, 10bl, 10mr, 11tr, 12t, 12m, 13br,
16br, 16–17t, 17tr, 19tl, 19mr, 24bl, 24–25b, 25m, 25br, 26–27, 28bl, 28tr.
ISOKON, PLUS, London: 14–15.
Popperfoto: 21br.
The Rural History Centre, University of Reading: 13t.
Science Photo Library, London: Christian Jegou/Publiphoto Diffusion (7r); 17mr.
Sotheby's Picture Library: 18tr.

Printed in the United States of America

1 2 3 4 5 6 7 8 9 06 05 04 03 02

SCIENCE FILES

materials

WOOD

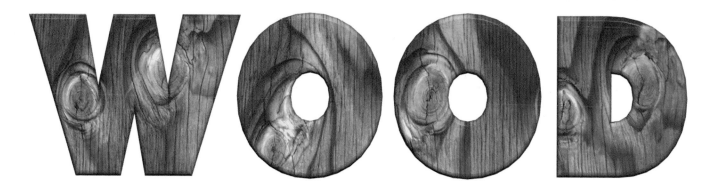

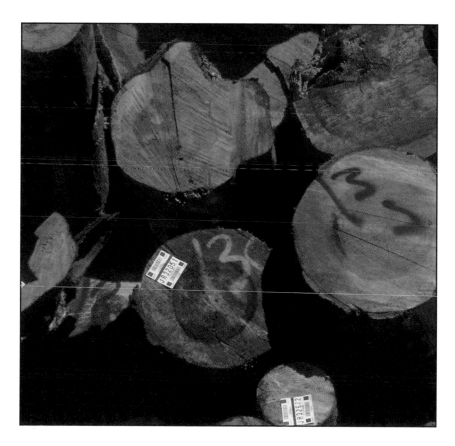

Steve Parker

Gareth Stevens Publishing
A WORLD ALMANAC EDUCATION GROUP COMPANY

CONTENTS

▲

When a tree is cut into logs, you can see circles, or rings, one inside the other. These were formed as the tree grew, one ring each year. How old was this tree?

INTRODUCTION

We use wood to make countless objects, from matchsticks to buildings and boats. We burn wood for light and warmth. We can also burn it to cook our food. We use it to create wonderful carvings, statues, and other works of art. We also alter, or process, wood to make paper, cardboard, rayon, resins, and many other materials and chemicals. A world without wood would be very different — and not only for us. Many animals also depend on trees and wood.

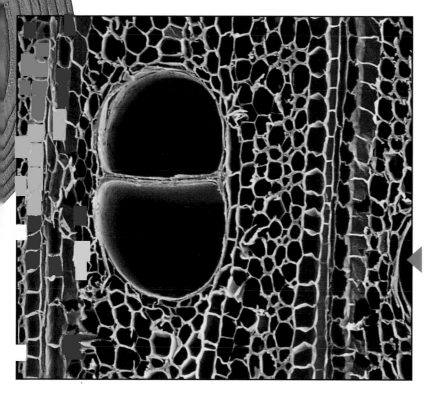

Wood is made of millions of tiny fibers and tubes. The fibers and tubes are made of two main substances, cellulose and lignin, with air spaces between them. This is why wood is light yet strong.

Houses, huts, sheds, and many other structures are made from wood. With proper care, they can last for generations.

Wood is mashed up and mixed with chemicals to make a thick "soup" called pulp. After pulp is pressed and rolled into sheets, it dries as paper.

WORLD OF WOOD

Woodlands and forests of various kinds cover about one-fifth of Earth's land surface. The trees in them vary greatly, and each type has special features and uses.

SOFTWOODS

Softwoods are trees with small, hard, thin, often needle-shaped leaves. They include pines, firs, spruces, and cedars. Because most of these trees keep their leaves all year-round, they are known as evergreens. Also, most of them grow their seeds in hard, woody cones and so are called coniferous trees, or conifers.

Forests take years to grow, but only hours to destroy.

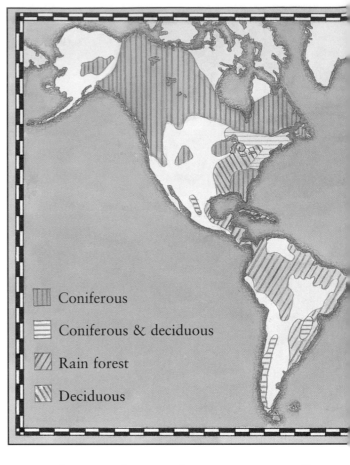

⦀	Coniferous
☰	Coniferous & deciduous
⧄	Rain forest
⧅	Deciduous

Rain forests thrive where it is wet all year (below). Those in warm places closer to the equator are tropical rain forests. They have more wildlife than anywhere else on Earth.

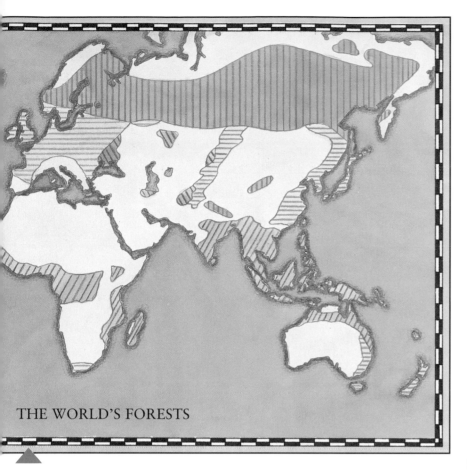

THE WORLD'S FORESTS

HARDWOODS

Most hardwood trees are strong and tough. Because they have wide, flat leaves, they are called broad-leaved trees. This group includes trees such as oaks, beeches, elms, and hickories. In some tropical places, hardwoods have leaves all year, so they are evergreen. But usually, their old leaves fall in autumn and new ones grow the next spring. Trees that lose and regrow leaves each year are called deciduous trees.

The main coniferous, or softwood, forests are in the northern lands. There, the winters are long, cold, and snowy. Deciduous woodlands and rain forests of various types usually contain many types of hardwood trees.

FACTS FROM THE PAST

Millions of years ago, there were no trees like the ones on Earth today. But there were huge plants, such as ferns, club mosses, and horsetails. The weather was warm and wet, and these plants grew in vast swamps. After they died, their remains were squashed and preserved, and they changed into the type of rock we call coal.

Swamps 300 million years ago

Around the world, millions of trees are cut down every day. New trees take many years to grow. We must plant millions more every day so we do not run out of wood.

TREE FARMS

Farmers grow many crops, like wheat, beans, and potatoes. Farming trees is similar to growing these other crops, except that trees are bigger and take years to grow. They begin as seeds taken from the parent tree. The science of growing and managing forests is known as forestry.

Many seeds begin to grow into baby trees, called seedlings, in greenhouses.

Seedlings grow into young trees called saplings, which are planted as a forest.

Each of these young trees has a plastic protector that keeps off frost and animals, such as deer and rabbits, that might nibble at the trees.

HOW FAST DO TREES GROW?

Most softwood trees grow faster than hardwood trees. After 20 years, a Scotch pine reaches 36 feet (11 meters) tall, but an oak is only 29.5 feet (9 m) high. The pine is fully grown and ready to cut down at 60 years old, while the oak is still growing at 100.

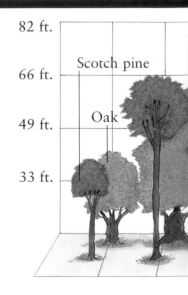

82 ft.

66 ft.   Scotch pine

49 ft.   Oak

33 ft.

20   30   40

MANY TREES, ALL THE SAME

Some trees, especially softwoods, are planted in vast forests filled with just one kind of tree. The trees grow fast and are similar in size and shape. These forests are known as monoculture stands. They produce lots of wood, but they are not very rich in wildlife.

LOTS OF DIFFERENT TREES

Other trees, especially hardwoods, grow in more natural woodlands that have many different kinds mixed together. The trees are cut at different times, when each one is ready. This produces less wood but creates homes for many wild animals.

IDEAS FOR THE FUTURE

Scientists are changing the genes in farm plants such as soybeans, corn, and tomatoes. These genetically modified versions are designed to grow bigger and faster. In the future, perhaps genetically modified trees will grow faster, stay healthier, and produce better wood.

A scientist altering genes

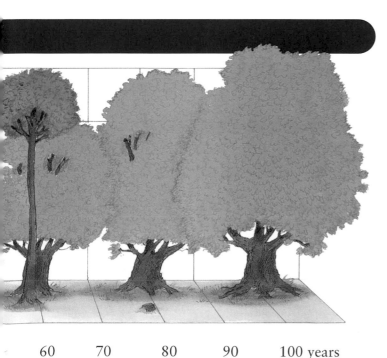

| 60 | 70 | 80 | 90 | 100 years |

This monoculture stand of softwood trees is ready to be harvested. Once they are cut down, new trees will be planted in their place.

HARVESTING WOOD

When trees are ready to be cut down, or felled, loggers move in with their chain saws and huge machines. In a few days, a whole forest can be cleared.

PATTERNS OF FELLING

In clear-cutting, all the trees in a forest are chopped down and the area is replanted. Seed-tree cutting uses a few trees left over in a clear-cut area to produce the seeds needed to replant the area naturally. In selection cutting, only a few trees of a certain size are felled each year.

Machines are used to rip bark and twigs from felled trees.

FACTS FROM THE PAST

For thousands of years, large animals have pulled and lifted massive logs from forests. In South Asia, trained elephants are still used for these tasks. They cause less damage to soil and plant life than huge, heavy trucks.

Asian elephants and mahouts (drivers)

AXES AND SAWS

Some trees are chopped down with axes, while others are sawed by hand. But most are cut with chain saws. The logger makes a sideways V-shaped cut in the trunk so that the tree falls in a certain direction. This causes the least damage to the tree itself and its neighbors.

Some trees and bushes are more useful when left alive. Lines of young trees with bendy wood, such as willows or hazels, are woven into "living fences."

HEAVY LOADS

Huge logs, such as tree trunks and thick branches, weigh many tons each. Large cranes and powerful trucks are needed to move them out of the forest and take them to the sawmills, paper mills, and other places where they will be processed.

Some logs may be floated out of the forest like huge rafts. However, most are hauled out by diesel trucks.

AT THE SAWMILL

Trees are living things, and each one grows slightly differently. So when logs arrive at the sawmill, they must be weighed, measured in size and shape, and examined for the quality of the wood and signs of disease.

In a modern sawmill, logs move along tracks ard are cut by whirling saw blades.

CHECKING THE QUALITY

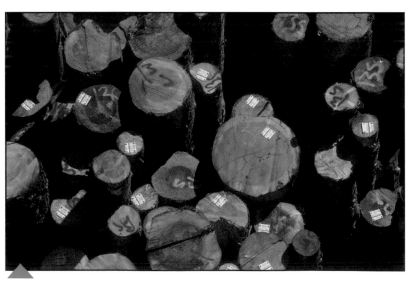

Logs that have been checked, ready for sawing

Logs from mixed forests are from many different types, shapes, and sizes of trees. As the logs arrive at the sawmill, lumber experts mark them with colored paints to show what type of wood they are and how they should be cut. Each sawing pattern makes different sizes and shapes of planks, strips, and blocks (*right*). Some logs have too many hard, dark areas, called knots, where branches grew from the original trunk. Knots spoil the strength and straightness of the wood, but they can look attractive, so they may be saved for decorative woodwork.

Trees grow fast in summer, producing light wood. They almost stop in winter, making a narrow dark band and creating growth rings.

WET WOOD

Fresh, or "green," wood from a recently felled tree has large amounts of water, sap, and natural juices inside it. If this wood is used too soon after being cut down, it may warp (bend), crack, and split as it dries. So, fresh wood must be carefully dried, or seasoned, before using.

SEASONED WOOD

To season wood naturally, whole or part-sawn logs are left in huge sheds with plenty of fresh air. Natural drying may take months, even years. Today, however, wood can be seasoned in hours by heating it in giant ovens, called kilns.

FACTS FROM THE PAST

Before there were motor-driven chain saws and sawmills, people cut logs by hand into boards and planks. They used long saws with handles at each end that were worked by two or more people.

Two-person pit saw (1920s)

Through and through

Radial quarter-sawn

Plain-sawn

Block quarter-sawn

Timber stacked for seasoning

13

MAKING NEW WOOD

Very few trees grow big enough to be sawn into large, flat sheets for walls, tables, or desktops. So, two or more smaller sheets or layers of wood are often joined or glued to make larger ones.

THE GRAIN OF WOOD

A piece of wood usually bends more easily in the direction that follows its grain — the way the tiny fibers in the wood form lines. Joining pieces of wood so that grains point in different directions gives more strength.

FACTS FROM THE PAST

Paper is made of tiny fibers from wood. Soak paper in water, and its fibers swell and loosen. Then mold and press the wet paper into a shape, add flour as a glue, and it will keep its new shape as it dries hard. This material is papier-mâché.

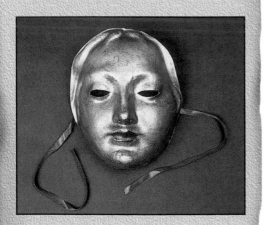

Papier-mâché theater mask

TYPES OF WOODEN BOARDS

PLYWOOD
Flat pieces of wood, called plies, are glued together with the grains of neighboring sheets at right angles to each other. This gives strength in both directions. Three-ply has three sheets, and so on.

BLOCKBOARD
This is a "sandwich" of long strips, or blocks, glued between two flat sheets. Like plywood, the sheet grains are at right angles to the block grains, for two-way strength.

PARTICLE BOARDS
Chipboards, fiberboards, hardboards, and similar sheets are made from small pieces of wood, pressed hard and glued or bonded together.

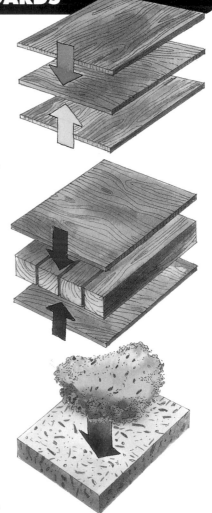

14

All of this furniture (left) is made from plywood. Plywood is made in many different thicknesses. If plies (layers) are dampened with steam, they can be bent around curved surfaces.

VENEERS

Veneers are thin sheets, or "leaves," of wood that are carefully shaved from a log and show the wood's grain and other patterns. Items made of cheap wood can be covered with a veneer to make them look beautiful.

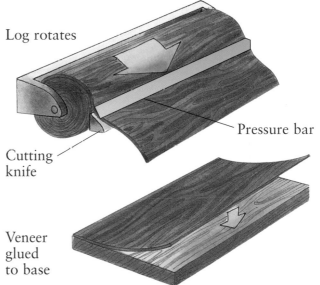

Log rotates

Pressure bar

Cutting knife

Veneer glued to base

MAN-MADE BOARDS

There are hundreds of different kinds of artificial, or man-made, boards. Each uses different kinds of wood pieces or different methods of joining the layers or pieces together. Chipboard is made from the small bits of wood that come from the sawmill and might otherwise be wasted. Fiberboard is made from wood soaked in chemicals that split the wood into tiny, hairlike fibers.

INSIDE AND OUT

Most man-made boards are used for making cupboards, furniture, walls, floors, and ceilings. Artificial boards used outdoors must be of good quality and made with wood and adhesives, or glues, that are not affected by rain, ice, or the hot, drying sun.

The veneer is carefully glued on.

WO KING WITH WOOD

Cutting, carving, joining, and trimming wood are some of the oldest crafts in the world. Each part of the world has its own traditional styles, depending partly on which trees grow there.

Bamboo is a grass, not a tree, but it has strong, woody, tube-like stems that can be used as scaffolding poles.

The sizes of the many beams in a house depend on the weight that they support.

WOODEN BUILDINGS

More than two-thirds of all wood is used for building houses, bridges, and similar structures. In areas with plentiful forests, timber is used for almost every part of a house, from the thick beams of the main framework to the flat shingles (tiles) on the roof. The wood is first treated with preservatives so it does not rot or soften and so wood-boring insects and other pests do not eat it away. Since fire is always a hazard in a wooden building, wood is sometimes also treated with chemicals that slow the spread of flames.

Joiners use many special tools.

FACTS FROM THE PAST

Modern power tools make woodworking easier, but most woodworkers still use hand tools. A lathe holds a piece of wood firmly and spins it around as its sharp blade, held against the spinning piece of wood, cuts the wood into a rounded shape. Old-fashioned lathes had foot pedals to spin the wood.

Working a manual lathe

WOODWORKING SKILLS

Carpenters work with most kinds of wood and wooden objects, especially large-scale structures. Joiners usually make smaller items, such as furniture and cupboards. Both carpenters and joiners need to choose the best type of wood for the job. Items that suffer a lot of wear and tear are usually made from oak and other hardwoods.

JOINING WOOD

There are dozens of ways of joining wood, from simply using glue or hammering in nails to carving complex shapes such as wedgelike dovetails. Each type of joint has its own special strengths. Joints do more than hold pieces of wood together. They show the woodworker's skills and make a wooden item much more valuable.

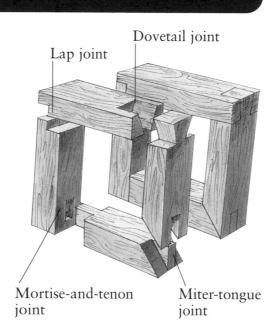

Lap joint

Dovetail joint

Mortise-and-tenon joint

Miter-tongue joint

Even high-tech concrete buildings rely on wood. The concrete is poured into a mold made from wooden boards, which are later removed.

BEAUTIFUL WOODS

No two pieces of wood are the same. The colors, patterns, lines of grain, and swirling knots are always slightly different. This means every wooden item, from a spoon to a huge table, is unique. Some of the world's most valuable objects are pieces of wooden furniture made by skilled craftspeople long ago.

Marquetry is made with thin wooden shapes assembled like a jigsaw puzzle.

FACTS FROM THE PAST

Some of the world's greatest works of art are wooden statues and carvings, and pictures, scenes, and designs cut into sheets of wood, known as woodcuts. One of the most famous artists who made woodcuts was Albrecht Dürer (1471–1528), a German painter and engraver.

Woodcut by Albrecht Dürer

MARQUETRY

Marquetry is making pictures from pieces of wood. Thin veneers of many wood types are carefully cut into shapes. They are fixed, or applied, to a base to create pictures and patterns.

MAKING WOODCUT PRINTS

Copies of pages can be made using woodcuts. First, the pictures and words are marked out.

Next, part of the marking is cut away. This leaves a raised design on the wood.

FINISHING WOOD

Wood that is bare or untreated gathers dust and dirt and may become marked with unsightly smears. Therefore, most wooden objects are finished to protect them. Many substances can be used for finishing. Polishes make wood smooth and shiny. They also "bring out" the grain and colors, making them stronger. Varnishes and lacquers also bring out the grain, and they protect the wood from chemicals, stains, and the effects of wear and tear.

Wood's color can be changed with special stains or dyes that soak into the wood, but still let the grain patterns show through.

Then, ink is rolled over the woodcut. The ink stays on the higher areas of the wood.

Paper is laid on the woodcut and pressed down. The ink sticks to the higher parts of

the wood. The paper is then peeled off to show the design in ink.

Native American totem poles are made from tree trunks carved with the shapes of animals, plants, and spirits.

CHEMICALS FROM WOOD

Not all trees that are cut down are used as whole wood. About one in every ten is processed, or altered, using pressure, powerful acids, heat, and solvents. The result is a wide range of chemicals and other products obtained from what started as wood.

Some artists' materials, such as charcoals and turpentine, are made from wood.

"DESTROYING" WOOD

To get chemicals from wood, the wood is shredded, heated, and attacked by solvents under great pressure. The wood breaks down, or dissolves, into a mushy soup. This is heated again in tall towers called columns.

At each stage, chemicals from the original wood are given off as gases, or evaporated, and then turned back into liquids in collecting tanks. Burning waste wood provides heat for the whole process.

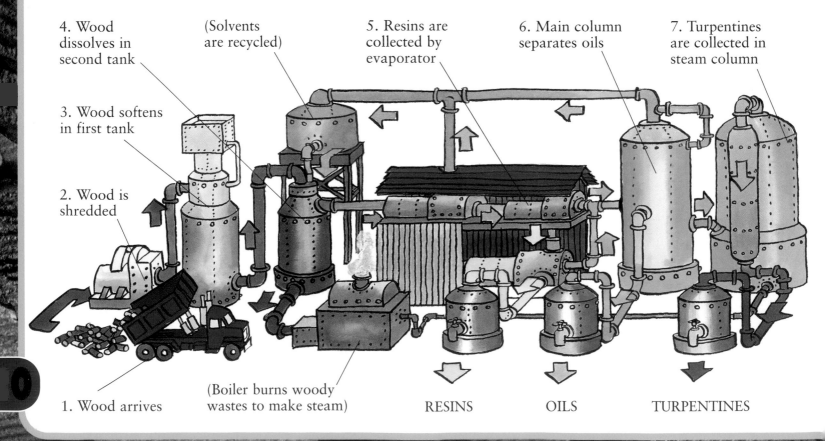

4. Wood dissolves in second tank

(Solvents are recycled)

5. Resins are collected by evaporator

6. Main column separates oils

7. Turpentines are collected in steam column

3. Wood softens in first tank

2. Wood is shredded

1. Wood arrives

(Boiler burns woody wastes to make steam)

RESINS   OILS   TURPENTINES

USEFUL WOOD CHEMICALS

The chemicals made from wood have many uses. Turpentines are used to thin paints and dissolve other chemicals. Resins and pitches are used to make glues and to preserve wooden objects like boats, fences, and sheds. Wood oils are used to make waterproofing substances, soaps, inks, and glues.

Gymnasts use a resin made from wood, called rosin, to give a good grip on the bars.

MORE WOODY CHEMICALS

About half of wood's weight is the substance cellulose. Cellulose is broken down by strong chemicals, such as acids and enzymes, to make sugars. These sugars can be made into molasses syrup to feed cattle, or yeast can be added to them to convert, or ferment, them into a type of alcohol called ethanol, which is used as a fuel in some cars and as a solvent.

FACTS FROM THE PAST

Before modern chemicals were developed, people obtained many of the substances they needed for daily life from nature — especially trees. Ancient Egyptians used chemicals obtained by heating wood to preserve dead bodies as mummies.

Animals skins are made into leather by tanning. Some chemicals for tanning come from tree bark, especially the bark of the black wattle tree.

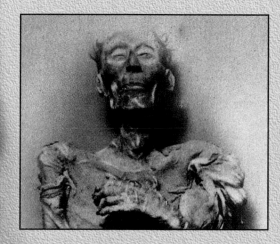

Ancient Egyptian mummy

21

CLOTHES FROM WOOD

Wood can be made into clothes, scarves, and other textile items! The substance cellulose, which makes up about half of wood's weight, is the basis for the artificial fiber known as rayon.

A NEW INVENTION

Most fibers are natural — cotton comes from cotton plants and wool comes from sheep. Rayon, which was invented in the 1880s, was the first artificial (man-made) fiber to be made. At first it was called artificial silk. In the 1920s, its name was changed to rayon and it became very popular. Its main raw material is — wood!

▲ *Clothes made from rayon are soft and flexible but also strong and long-lasting.*

MAKING RAYON

To make rayon, wood chips are pulped into a "soup" with solvents and other chemicals. Cellulose forms a separate layer in the pulp and is poured or skimmed off. Cellulose sheets are the main raw material for rayon. The cellulose is heated with caustic soda. It breaks into flakes, which are then added to another chemical called carbon disulphide.

5. Viscose is aged and cleaned

1. Sheets of cellulose soaked in caustic soda

2. Sheets broken into flakes

3. Flakes mixed with carbon disulphide

4. Caustic soda mixed in to make viscose

USES OF RAYON

Today, rayon fabric is less popular, since there are many other artificial fibers. But it is fairly cheap and easy to make, so it is still produced in regions with plenty of spare wood. Rayon also has other uses besides clothing. It forms the ropelike strengthening cords inside tires. And because it soaks up, or absorbs, liquids well, it is used for medical pads and bandages.

This is viscose before it is squirted through spinnerets to make rayon.

IDEAS FOR THE FUTURE

Rayon was widely used until the 1940s, when nylon became popular. But nylon is made partly from oil (petroleum). If crude oil supplies ever run low, we might go back to making more rayon.

Nylon may run out one day.

This mixture, called viscose, is left for a few days to "age." After cleaning it to remove wastes and air bubbles, the viscose is squirted through tiny holes, known as spinnerets, into a vat of liquid sulphuric acid. In the acid, the viscose turns into the flexible strands that we call rayon.

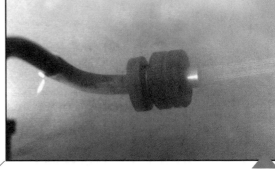

Rayon strands emerging from spinnerets

Pump

6. Viscose vacuum treated to remove air bubbles

7. Viscose forced through spinnerets into sulphuric acid bath

8. Rayon yarn wound on spools

PRODUCTS FROM TREES

In addition to wood and chemicals, trees provide many other products. Some are collected from trees growing in forests. Others are obtained from the wood or other parts of the tree, using complicated methods.

Charcoal kilns, Malawi

Extracts of ginkgo (maidenhair tree) are in this gel. The shampoo contains oil from palm trees.

RUBBER

All rubber originally came from trees. Today, there are many different kinds of artificial, or man-made, rubber. But natural rubber is still used to make certain things, such as tires for airplanes and other vehicles.

Natural rubber is soft, flexible, and elastic. It comes from trees such as the hevea (rubber tree). A small cut is made in the tree's bark. Milky liquid sap, called latex, seeps into a cup fixed to the tree. This is called rubber tapping. Latex is two-thirds water, so it must be processed to make pure rubber.

OILS AND EXTRACTS

For thousands of years, people have used natural oils from trees. These are often based on sap, a liquid that is like a tree's "blood," carrying minerals and nutrients around inside the tree. Oil may also be taken, or extracted, from a tree's leaves, fruits, seeds, or nuts. Some oils and extracts are used as medicines. They are put into ointments, pills, or vapors. Others are used simply because they have a pleasing smell!

Not all woods are used for their strength. The cork tree has light wood with many air spaces in it. It is used to make stoppers for bottles.

Natural rubber comes from plantations of rubber trees (below). Latex is hung out as sheets to dry (inset). It is later used for soft products such as surgeons' gloves.

FACTS FROM THE PAST

Ancient people believed that the hard, shiny, golden substance called amber was made from the rays of the setting Sun. In fact, amber is sticky, liquid sap or resin that, long ago, oozed from a cut in a tree's bark. It hardened and sealed the cut. Lumps of amber are preserved as fossils from prehistoric times. Some contain small animals that got trapped in the stickiness millions of years ago.

An insect trapped in amber

25

MAKING PAPER

The paper this page is made of was once part of a tree. About one-tenth of all trees are specially grown to be mashed into a souplike pulp by machines and chemicals and made into paper and cardboard. It is a long and complex industrial process that uses huge amounts of chemicals and energy.

Papyrus from Ancient Egypt

FROM WOOD . . .   TO PULP . . .

Pulp is made from freshly cut logs — and also old paper, cardboard, wood chips, rags, and many other waste or recycled materials.

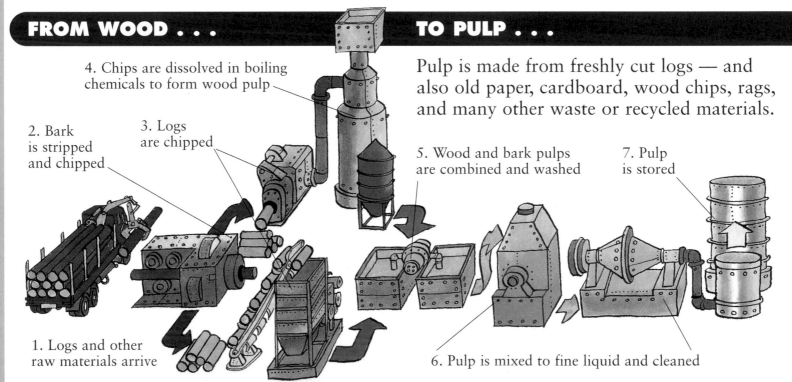

4. Chips are dissolved in boiling chemicals to form wood pulp

2. Bark is stripped and chipped

3. Logs are chipped

5. Wood and bark pulps are combined and washed

7. Pulp is stored

1. Logs and other raw materials arrive

6. Pulp is mixed to fine liquid and cleaned

Nearly all paper is made from softwood trees grown for this purpose. They are much less expensive than hardwood trees and their fibers are longer.

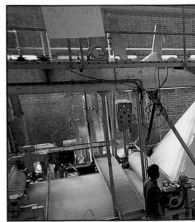

FIBERS AND SHEETS

The fibers of cellulose are held together by another substance called lignin. When wood is pulped, the lignin is removed or dissolved, so that the fibers become loose and separate. They are then mixed with various liquids and chemicals, and spread out as large layers on rollers. As the layers are pressed thinner and heated, the fibers flatten together and dry. The thinnest products of this process are sheets of paper. Thicker card material, or even thicker cardboard, are also made in this way.

. . . TO PAPER

Pulp is mixed with bleaching chemicals to make white paper or with dyes for other colors. The headbox spreads out the pulp as a wide layer on a wire-mesh belt. The pulp layer is pressed, heated, rolled, and treated with chemicals before it becomes paper.

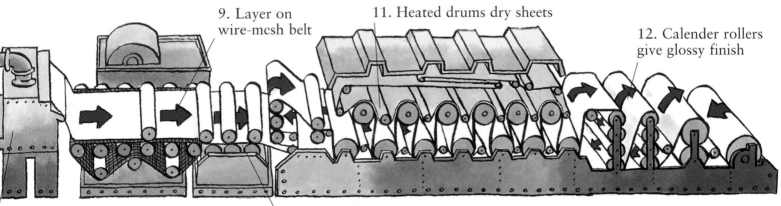

9. Layer on wire-mesh belt

11. Heated drums dry sheets

12. Calender rollers give glossy finish

8. Headbox spreads pulp

10. Press rollers squash layer into thin sheet

Sheets of paper on the press are a few feet (m) wide and miles (km) long (left). They are cut into smaller rolls to take to printers and other users (right).

27

WOOD FOR THE FUTURE

A forest that is destroyed by fire can take 100 years to grow back again.

Wood will remain a vital material — but not only for houses, furniture, paper, and other products. The trees grown for wood give food and shelter to animals. They also give out the oxygen we need to breathe and hold soil so it is not washed or blown away. Trees are essential to our world!

Firewood is scarce in many countries. If new trees are not planted, the supplies of wood will run out one day.

PLANT MORE TREES!

In some parts of the world, new trees are planted to replace the trees we cut down. In these places, wood is a renewable resource. But in other parts of the world, forests are cut down for timber; then the soil is used for a few years for crops; then as grazing for farm animals; then — nothing. No new trees are planted for future use. The bare soil washes or blows away. This kind of destruction happens especially in tropical rain forests.

As well as planting more trees, we can use the trees and wood we already have in better ways. Rare hardwood timbers such as teak and mahogany should come from forests that are sustainable. This means new trees are planted as old ones are felled. We can recycle paper and wooden items and reuse wood itself in many ways.

This used paper is ready for recycling.

This symbol is used to show products that are made from recycled materials.

1. Newspapers, glossy paper (magazines), and cardboard are collected and separated into the correct paper bins.

2. Paper for recycling is collected from the bins, pressed into bales, and taken to the paper mill.

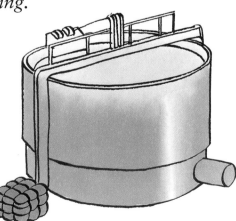

3. The bales are put into a hydrapulper. The pulp is used to make products such as paper towels.

WOODS AND THEIR USES

	TYPE OF WOOD	FEATURES AND USES
HARDWOODS	Beech	Smooth, hard, and fairly strong; used for boxes, flooring, furniture, woodcuts, frames, handles, shafts
	Elm	Strong, irregular grain; used for furniture, boat building
	Hickory	Coarse, wavy grain; used for tool handles, sports equipment
	Mahogany	Dark and hard; used for carvings, panels, furniture, instruments
	Maple	Light, straight-grained; used for furniture, joinery, veneers, musical instruments, floorboards, wall panels, plywood
	Oak	Pale and tough; used for furniture, joinery, outdoor woodwork
	Teak	Uneven grain, oily; used for joinery, outdoor furniture, veneers
SOFTWOODS	Walnut	Dark with distinctive grain and knots; used for furniture, carving, veneers, cabinets and joinery, gun stocks (handles)
	Cedar	Scented, fairly soft, but long-lasting; used for chests, boxes, houses, roofing
	Cypress	Durable, long-lasting; used for doors, window frames
	Fir	Obtained in large, knot-free sizes; used for buildings, plywood and other boards, walls, poles, some joinery and furniture
	Hemlock	Even, straight, prominent grain; used for construction and in buildings, plywood, joinery
	Larch	Straight, pale, and tough; used for beams, props, boat planks
	Pine	Even and close-grained; used for doors, tables, chairs, cabinets
	Sequoia	Grain varies from fine to stringy; used for roofs, walls
	Spruce	Pale and even; used for joinery, musical instruments, boxes
	Yew	Hard, long-lasting; used for furniture, joinery, handles, shafts

cellulose: a material that makes up about half the weight of wood. It contains small fibers, linked end to end like beads on a necklace.

clear-cutting: to fell all of the trees in a forest. The area is usually then replanted.

dissolve: to mix thoroughly with a liquid and form a solution.

grain: the markings, pattern, or texture of the fibers in wood.

hardwood: the dense, hard wood from a tree that has leaves and flowers. Oak, ash, and maple are hardwoods.

lignin: a material in wood that holds the cellulose fibers in wood together.

rayon: an artificial fiber made from cellulose.

resin: a sticky substance in a tree's bark and wood. It protects the tree from pests and seals cuts in the bark.

sap: the liquid that carries minerals and nutrients through plants.

seed-tree cutting: to chop down most of the trees in a forest, leaving some standing to produce seeds that grow into new trees.

softwood: the wood from a tree that has needle-like leaves all year-round and grows its seeds in cones. Pine is one kind of softwood.

solvent: a substance that is used for dissolving other substances.

MORE BOOKS TO READ

America's Forests. Earth Watch series. Frank Staub (Carolrhoda Books)

Early Loggers and the Sawmill. The Early Settler Life Series. Peter Adams, Bobbie Kalman (Crabtree Publishing)

Wood. Would You Believe It series. Catherine Chambers (Raintree/ Steck-Vaughn)

Woodworking for Kids: 40 Fabulous, Fun and Useful Things for Kids to Make. Kevin McGuire (Lark Books)

WEB SITES

Papermaking Process. http://www.ppic.org.uk

What Tree Is It? http://www.oplin.lib.oh.us/products/tree

Due to the dynamic nature of the Internet, some web sites stay current longer than others. To find additional web sites, use a reliable search engine with one or more of the following keywords: *forests, hardwoods, logging, papermaking, rayon, rubber, softwoods, trees, woodcuts, woodworking.*

INDEX